MY BAD TEMPER

Written by Dan Carr

Pictures by Bartholomew and Bill Clark

CONCORDIA PUBLISHING HOUSE · SAINT LOUIS

Manufactured in Shenzhen, China/055760/414399

17 18 19 20 21 22   24 23 22 21 20 19

Dear God,

I am talking to You from my room.
I am being punished by Mom and Dad.
I need Your help, God, because
I have a very …

bad temper.

When I got up this morning, I could not find one of my shoes. I was angry because I was scared Mom would be angry at me for losing it. So I **punched** my little brother. I thought he had hidden my shoe on purpose.

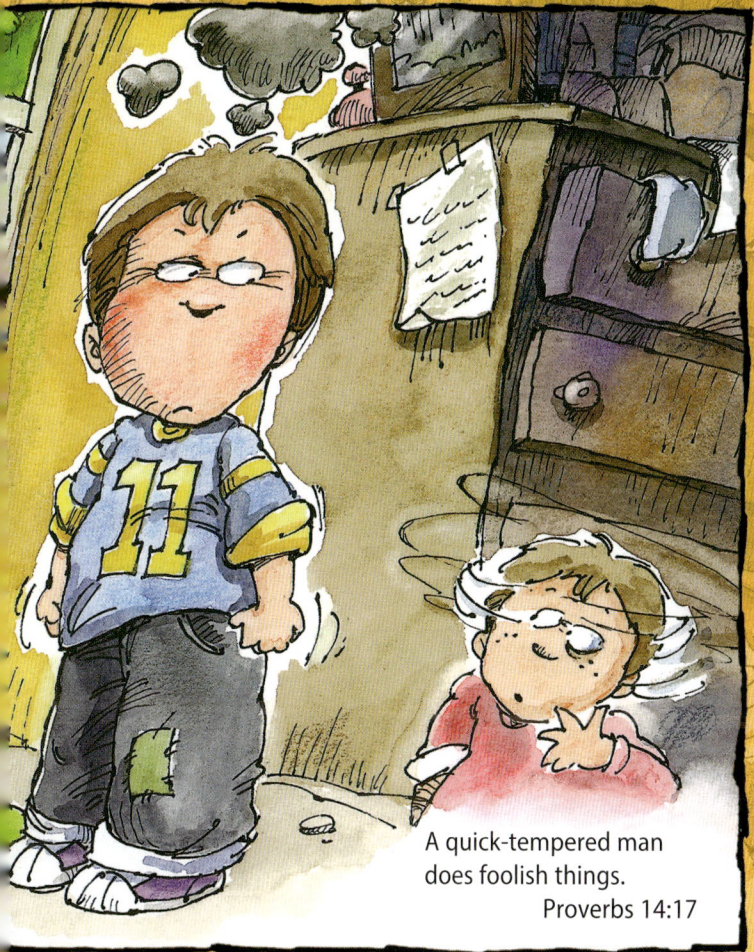

A quick-tempered man
does foolish things.
Proverbs 14:17

Then, for breakfast,
Mom made oatmeal.
She knows **I hate oatmeal.**
She never makes what I like.
So I **shoved** the bowl away
and spilled the milk.

Later, I could not find my bucket
that I use to lift things into my tree house.
So I **punched** my little brother again.
He smiles when Mom says that I am not
careful. I hate it when Mom thinks
that my brother is better than I am.

When I am afraid, I will trust in You.
Psalm 56:3

When Dad came home,
he would not take me fishing
as he had promised. **I slammed the door.**
That is when Mom and Dad
took me to my bedroom.

We talked about what happened.

My shoe was in my closet,
where I had thrown it.

My bucket was in the garage,
where I had filled it with things
to take to the tree house.

And Dad wanted to go fishing,
but he had a meeting.

Then Mom and Dad said,
"We know you want to be
nicer, but sometimes you are
so afraid that you get angry."
They told me that I **never**
have to be afraid that they don't
love me or that You, God, don't love me.

Whoever comes to Me
I will never drive away.
John 6:37

So, here I am, Jesus.
I am really sorry for what I did.
Teach me to remember that
my family really does **love me**
and **forgives me,** just as **You do.**
Help me show others
how much **love** I have,
especially my little brother. Amen.